Promise of the Rainbow
Through My Tears

Promise of the Rainbow Through My Tears

RICHARD CLAUDE VALDEZ

Aperture

Poems

Richard Claude Valdez

Published, 2009 by Trafford

Aperture is a collection of poems drawn from life experiences and reflected through the emotional lens of love, joy, pain, disappointment, anguish, loneliness and exhilaration.

Order this book online at www.trafford.com
or email orders@trafford.com

Most Trafford titles are also available at major online book retailers.

Printed in the United States of America.

ISBN: 978-1-4269-6358-2 (sc)
ISBN: 978-1-4269-6359-9 (e)

Trafford rev. 06/17/2011

 www.trafford.com

North America & International
toll-free: 1 888 232 4444 (USA & Canada)
phone: 250 383 6864 ♦ fax: 812 355 4082

To my Siblings

Acknowledgement

Cover photos by Sylvie Beauchesne

Interior photos by Richard Claude Valdez

CONTENTS

A Song to My Father

Unheralded!
He walked along his ways,
Quiet footsteps kept rhythm with his greying days.
Spoke ill of no one, laid claim to nothing,
Except his blessing-
Tolling as the bells on Sunday morning.

He turned a corner,
        Changed a lane.
Moved in the sunlight,
        Wept in the rain.
He bowed to the green hills,
        Marched onto the plain.
Swung his shoulders westward,
        Ever homeward again.

Unheralded!
He strode along his quiet path.
His thoughtful countenance harboured no wrath.
He spawned no fight, stoked no quarrel,
But wrestled with his thoughts,
Moving with the breezes on the hill.

He sat in silence
        Upright in his chair,
His eyes towards heaven,
        Many burdens to bear.
His lips moved in quiet
        As he mumbled a prayer,
Then raised himself up
        To attend to our care.

Unheralded!
Unarmed!
A soldier on guard,
As we children ran circles in the quiet front yard.
Then he rose with the sunrise,
In the west ran his blood,
Through the long legged darkness as aged Samson he stood.

He rose one grey morning,
        Kissed us all on the cheek.
Took his place with the mourning,
        Shook hands with the meek.
To rest on the Sabbath,
        With Bible in hand,
Took his space in the Graveyard,
        With brothers to stand.

Now he lights at our window,
        Stands guard at our door.
Points the way to the heavens,
        All together once more!
His smile is the sunrise,
        He calls from the west.
He beckons his children,
        To the garden of rest.

After the Performance

He rose with dawn breaking,
With faint memory remembering an evening.

There was something missing:
A sadness lurking
A journey ending.

Something took place yesterday that left an awkward void-
Food without the taste.
The drum still echoes someplace
In space.

Wedged between the tombstone and marble-
Buried in the graveyard of journeys:
The first bar
Second system
The crescendo
Largo
The dead baton
Final movement
The rest
The threnody
Dirge
Elegy.

As A Lad

As a lad with my Dad
I left for school one day.
He held my hand along the way;
We dreamt dreams of youth and age.
Thoughts after, I returned all grey
But without him at my blushing hand.
Along the dream he had to stay
Somewhere between my sleep and wake.

Now I join him on a similar day-
Sunny and warm; we take
The same walk taken dreams away.
He takes my withered hand to join with his:
Mine all old and worn
With burr and thorn-
Old blood and bone
From being caught between the angry stone.

His touch I remember!
All safe and tight
Secured in might,
In time when I was pink as a plum.

He smiles.
So much younger now–
Scarce line on his kind brow;
Eyes with light not there before
He closed the door.

He holds me tight we join in flight.

A boy once more, my lessons learnt
And deeds all burnt;

I sleep sweet sleep tonight.

Autumn Dance

The gentle hum of the wind from an unpretentious chord,
The pluck from the harp of a new born twig,
Orange-red notes that score across the ledger lines of autumn;
Burning a treble clef in coloured tones-
An overture to autumn's symphony.

And the first brave leaf begins her Fall
With a gentle reluctant *Glissade*,
Looking back longingly at an umbilical stem
Severed by the season's efficient midwife-
Fingers stained in the red blood of autumn's birth.

A final *Arabesque!*
A *Chasse* along the cold pathway.
Then a gentle *Glissade*
Graceful and sad,
To a final cry with the wind-
A gasped *"Jete!"*
Then, *Bras Croise*

In solitary Finale-
She succumbs to the autumn's coloured weaves,
Drowning in the season of leaves.

Before He Takes Us Under

Before he takes us under
The Undertaker turns us over
To the butcher's block in the corner

And with scalpel saw and hammer
He removes the liver

And then begins to sever
All that was a- tether

Like leg of lamb or mutton
He dumps us near the chopper

Where once we had a belly button
Soon we'll have a zipper

Then rearranges our bowels
With chisel saw and trowels

Then pumps us full of liquid
That puffs us up all stupid

Then sutures to our humps and rump
Before he fires up the pump

Then comes the intravenous
To our shameless sagging anus

Then he proceeds to paint our face
And dress us in some fancy lace

In which some other bloke was dressed
Just before he became abscessed

Then adorned in Sunday best
Our entwined hands across our chest

Now we look like mannequins
Clasped hands praying for our sins

A clown on public display
While the pretentious pious pray

Where no one really wants to stay
On this inconvenient day

Then after guests have had their fill of mourning
He strips us of fine array of clothing

Then final thrust to our stuffed-up rump
On this our last and farewell dump

A lid
A nail
A clasp

A clang
A bolt
A thud

A tap
A snap
A final slap

As the carcass springs the trap!

Let loose the anxious worms to feast
We are gone a- flying to the East.

Burnt Toast

Burnt toast.
The smell of comfort
On Sunday mornings
Alone,
Contented.

Coffee black and hot builds a cloud of steam-
A spiralled dream
Of years ground to grit
Like sand in the hour-glass spit.

Pyjamas, sleepy and warm with the smell of dreams,
A premature resurrection of gentle contentedness
For life before the long sleep.

The dark brown toast-
Sunday morning's roast
A testimony to life curled in a favourite chair-
Hardly thinking.

Dreaming awakened dreams.
Stunned in silence.

A scented sentence.

A gentle penance.

Purring like the family feline.

Burnt toast.
Sacramental Host.

Call to a Boy

Where do you go when the night is falling
Where do you hide when the cold winds gnaw
Where do you 'bide when the snows are blowing
     -Along the hedges and out on the moor
     -Along the hedges and out on the moor

Where do you go when the winds are howling
Where do you rest in the cold frost hoar
Where do you nest when the sleet is flying
     -Under the benches at cold mission door
     -Under the benches at cold mission door

You can come home the door is still open
From break of dawn to grey dusky ev'en
No longer roam all past now forgiven
-Lay down your burden and wander no more
-Lay down your burden and wander no more

Where do you go when the leaves are falling
Where do you lay when the cold rains pour
Where do you pray when all hope is failing
     -Deep in the ditches from cold winters roar
     -Deep in the ditches from cold winters roar

Where do you weep when your heart is broken
Where do you creep in the damp spring thaw
Where do you sleep when the grass is frozen
     -Under the bridges on cold city floor
     -Under the bridges on cold city floor

You can come home my arms are still open
From stormy sea to warm sunny shore
No longer roam the spell is now broken
-Lay down your burden and wander no more
-Lay down your burden and wander no more

What do you see now your eyes are dimming
Where do you lay now you breathe no more
Who do you call now your voice is fading
      -Aye! Call me, me laddie we'll part never more
      -Aye! Call me, me laddie we'll part never more

We'll find peace in the valley me laddie e'er more,
In the green green valley me laddie e'er more.

Cardinal Cardinalis

A crimson gash
That curls in the summer heat.
    A fluted splash
On tarantella feet.
    He stings the evening's dusk with a flint of crimson.

On his throne of green,
    Regal robes once more
In my garden scene.

Under the shade of evening's dusk
    He feeds alert and poised-
Looking at me, chained in wonder.

"Have I intruded you feathered God"
    " Upon your sacred sod"?
As I in humble nod
    Now suck your hallowed sight.

With pirouetted dance he bids, "So long!"
In full-throated Cardinalis song,
And tumbles home-
Red angel in the sunset's dome.

Chaud'eau

To rise when dawn is deep in sleep
Sky slate and grey in colour,
     When Moon is shy
In her lover's sky
     I boil with the sea's salt fever.

To chase the Mackerel out to sea
To race the dawn away,
     And down the rum
With the lapping hum
     Of the waves from the bow and spray.

I kiss the women on the cheek
And taste their full red lips,
     But the sea calls
With her raw squalls
     And I long for her salted hips

With line and hook and gaff all stored
I turn to greet the sea,
     My heart beats fast
As it climbs the mast
     -To the waves to the wind and me.

Her dance her pitch her heave her yaw
To salt and spume and swell,
     Sweet lover's taste
Pitch rising waist
     I drive to the depths of her well.

Farewell my love please do not weep-
She rolls me in her dance,
        To feel her heave
I cannot leave
        I drown in the depths of her trance.

December 1998

On this barren December day,
When the chill of winter's will lay buried
In the lukewarm blood of autumn's song;
When the tree birds, weary and anxious-
Wild in their wildness and confused in their confusion
Flutter in loops
Silent in swoops
Scatter their brown feathers on the naked grass;

I lay my life in measured:
  When?
   Why?
    And wherefore?

On this bare bosom of winter's dawning breath-
I crouch within the webbed corners of white waiting
For that final brown leaf of autumn to crash down
Upon my welcoming heart.

Do Not Admire Me!

Do not admire me,
Love me!
Only roses bloom to be admired.

Break my heart!
But do not admire me;
For the pain of a broken heart testifies that it once travelled.

Teared and torn
Threadbare and worn
It bares its scars for all to see-
Like nails in the hands of sacrifice.

A heart once loved cries out with the song of sweet tenderness;
It sings in the heavens,
It fulfills its being.

But an admired heart languishes in the darkness of sombre
yesterdays.

It lurks like a wraith in the graveyards of dead dreams.
It lies abandoned, aborted and absent.
It remains:
Barren
Untried
Untested
Unrequited
Unloved
Inutile
Futile and worthless.

Love me!
And leave the admiration to the cowardly and the craven.

Drunk at the Pub

A draught of dark beer in my glass
A crude hewn chair to rest my arse
A note of music stains my ear
No welcome cheek to trace my tear
Dark beer
A chair
A note an ear
A glass
My arse
An eye a tear
Now watch me tumble down the stair
It matters not you cheer my dear
There's no one here or there to care
Shet 'em up ! Lesh 'ave 'nosher beer

First Light

First light of day
Burns its way from heaven;
Shadows in haste
Flee from sunlight's ray.
The earth stands up-
Caught by light
Shakes free itself from sleep
And with a shawl of light wipes dry the morning's dew.

The early birds take flight,
Freed from the sheltered night;
The rose unfolds its arms,
Then come the busy bees to light upon the yawning nectar
farms.

A new day psalm,
First Light!

Footsteps

Footsteps are all some folk possess
They have no thoughts to call their own
No deed no voice no word by them is sown
Just footsteps.
Without the print
Without a hint
That they have ever been
A part of this thankless scene
They leave their footsteps as they leave their smell
Perhaps stronger at a spot where once they fell
What they have left behind none can tell
Except footsteps.
Along a dark and an empty street
Across a deep damp meadow
Worn out feet
Keeping time with the river's flow
Footsteps numbering the rain drops pour
Today a little more
Tomorrow even less
Footsteps are all some folk possess.

From My Bedroom Window

From my bedroom window-
Disconsolate,
I watch the Autumn bleed
And the woeful weeping Willow wail silently.

Her mate the mighty Maple stands guard;
A wise old money lender
Exchanging green for leaves of gold;
Knowingly wise that time will bring
Fresh harvest in the Spring.

But what of Spring?
A new beginning?
A continuing?
Neither guaranty
Nor certainty;
As inexorable old age in loose law of whim and will-
Void of compassion,
Bends my bones in his own fashion.

The window closes,

The curtains drawn-
Closing out the ever limping clock of seasons.

Now I turn to greet my shadow,
My hands he bids me bind.
He leads and I must follow
Along the trails of sorrow.
With broken branches left behind
Down falling steps into a veiled tomorrow.

Her First Death

It was her first death this death so true
     For death she never knew.
It was her first death on this day of penitence
     And she in milk white innocence
Prepared to face the gloom.

Under the veil of blissful unknowing
     After a dark cloud leaned against her sun.
And her gloom in a trough of torrents
     Laid her in Baptismal font.

It was a strange shaped pain
     That left no mark nor blood nor stain,
For it was deeper in the depths of soul
     Under the layered folds it stole.

A pain that worked its way to salted vein
     And there to fester and remain;
As boil within the flesh contain
     But still in loss her love sustain-

Deep within her memory lain
Her father's love will never wane.

I Hear the Sounds of Children's Laughter

I hear the sounds of children's laughter
    Rise like smoke above the trees,
Those gentle gleeful shrieks of joy
    That's carried on a breeze.
And with a feathered hush to lie
    Between a childhood sigh,
As butterfly on scented flower
    Alights on sacred bower.

What cause such sounds of sweet delight
    To roam from innocence?
And where they play between the hush
    In still and quiet silence.
"There! It rises once again!"
    A shriek and mix of laughter,
Like showers from a gentle rain
    And arrows from a heartfelt quiver.

I hear the sounds of childhood's laughter
    Sweet gurgles from a brook,
Incantations unrehearsed-
    Lilies in a garden nook.
At times on bright and sunny day
    When I am all alone,
I imitate their sound of laughter
    And listen for their tone.

I wait

Spring dies in a veil of regrets.

Under the thick heavy snow he hides from me;
As the green of summer hides
Secluded beneath the bleak gelid heel of winter.

And autumn, an orange teardrop covered in sadness.

With each moan and shadow,
Each blade of wayward light
And whispering sigh
And groan,
Each shuffled step
And turn of bolt
And lock.

Still I wait.

Through lazy dawns
And lonely clawing night,
Through days when the sun stands tall in the sky-
That ever seeing eye of Horus
Blind to my plight.

Yet I wait.

In the dream of memory and in the rhythm of rolling thought-

The more I wait!

Each Sunday morning the belfry from the old church across the
winding street
Rings the hour ten-
Calling me to service; too late to a time now spent.

Gongs like steel hammers,
Hammering the nails through bare bone
To brittle bare and powdered chalk;
Imbedding rusted time deep down through memories festered
sore-
Primed with pain and pus and pulse of times merciless march;
Reminding gloom, that dark obsidian torrent
Will soon in endless flow break the dykes
And flood the green valley with mud and moss and mould
And moribund waste.

Even then I wait.

He never came:

This beat of my heart
This eye of my sight
This red of my blood
This marrow of my bone
This melody of my soul
This rhythm of my pulse
This volley of my breath
This God of my adoration
This salt of my tears

This Angel wrapped in Apocalyptical Scroll,
This executioner of my soul.

If When

If when the mowing claw of winter shines my bare brittle bones
to milk white chalk

If when the warm hearted sun trades his light for the dark crotch
of night

If when my lover falls willingly within the arms of a long treasured
friend

If when the young child in sooth and youth and youthful in
innocence pokes out my eyes

If when the old, stooped in years, weary in thought and scabbed
with age defiles me with curses

If when the dog-toothless without claw, mange to the bone, rife
with ticks and sore chews my calf as I go by

If when my ears go blind, my touch fails to taste and my eyes
abort sweet melody for the grunts of wild boars

If when I can rise from my bed sweet with sweat and fragrant
with the bouquet of my own urea-

Can still haul myself up on two bowed legs and smile;

Then I have earned the honour to have lived
        And my reward to die.

If!

If I knew then
What I know now?
I would have known when
I would have known how:
Now & then
When & how
-To unleash the pen
And soften the brow.

If Only

If only we could see
          around the swirling bend.
If only we could dance
          at the curve of life.
If only we could lie
          at the lip of circumstance.
If only we could savour
          the edge of experience.
If only we could grasp
          the crack of opportunity.
If only we could love
          in Love's absence.
If only we could be!
          Without being.
If only!

It Is Over.

It is over,

It is over:

An empty Cruse

A withered flower

The dying light in a darkened bower

The broken lamp from a crumpled tower

The burnt out fuse has spent its power

The sickly wave at last must flounder

The Muse's gold to tarnished copper

The empty flask to fellow rover

A last fair breath has lost its shoulder

Oh God! The storm-

 A heart in thunder!

The angels light now torn asunder

Her debt is paid for freedom's hunger

The green eyed maid alone must linger

It is over

It is over!

Just Before the Rains Came

Just before the rains came down in sheets and shafts of spears-
Breezes curled its legs around the flowered garden bed
And lifted skirts of leaves and shrubs to peer beneath the soft
white petals,
And kiss the lips of nectar folds that lay invitingly mysterious.

Then Roses spread their thorny branches
And opened wide their bright red petals
For wind in slow sweet waltz to reach in-
Unencumbered.

Then flowers roused in essence stance
Begin their rolling waving dance,
And stem before the rain, once limp and soft
Stands up so taught and straight aloft.

And all the garden now entrusts
The wind to enter in with gusts,
And all the bush and shrub and flower
-The Rose and Lilly and Lavender-
Released its redolent aroma
To welcome anxious rain to enter.

And the rains came long and deep and hard
Within the scented garden yard.

Lost

Fur and bone shot from the forest green-
Launched in frozen bone and fur,
Landing scared upon the sidewalk with the
Startled eyes of an infant.

Collared in bells,
Leathered and collared,
Claws in staccato-
Ticking with the rhythm of a nervous clock
On a face of stone.

"Clam!" She called.
A voice from the dark woods-
Hysteria trapped in a single note,
A cappella drowned deep in concern.

He trotted passed my legs with a grin of fear.
An arched head to savour a stranger's smell,
Doggedly reaching unfamiliar territory.

"Clam!" She called again-
This time with a tremor.

I knelt to one knee and opened a palm,
A gesture to insure that I meant him no harm.
He looked into my eyes and questioned!
And with an unsteady gait
Bolted for the street corner straight.

Amid the merciless engines and songs of horns
He emerged unscathed:

Lifted his head,
Stopped,
Sniffed,
Panted,
Whimpered,
And headed west,
Lost in maze -zigzag –crisscross- confusion.

"Clam!"
A dead voice from a dead past faded away above the trees:
Mixed with the hail of horn
The tear of tyre
Thud of bone and metal torn
Fur and blood and funeral pyre.

MacKenzie

I do not know you little one-
Born of the sunflower.
You live far away on the other side of life
Where *childhood* dances to the rhythm of angels.

You came in quietly like a "day's eye"-
A brightly coloured daisy bathed in a face of florets,
Pushing through the summer's dawn-
A bright smiling face rising up to greet us.

I never saw your smile gentle soul,
But heard them call you-*MacKenzie!*
A Gaelic song of *fire born,*
Such a large sound for a tiny mound,
Just a handful of feathers soft and round.

They say your smile came up like the sun
And opened the sky with a slice of dawn,
And your laugh sprouted in a gurgle of waves,
Kissing the welcoming sand.

You bounced up with the legs of a fawn
And skipped with a sigh of wind that rushed to a welcoming
cheek-
Heather and Hyacinth and Roses and Lilies,
Scents of young souls fresh from the stars.

"MacKenzie,
Stay for a while!
Just a little longer,
So I can see your smile

And hear your song of "Unfettered love and innocence:"
Do not be in such haste to join your mates in chorus of Cherubs.

You see, my steps are strewn with the brown of late Autumn,
Yours are piled with the green of Summer-
Fresh precocious lips in a kiss of daisies.

MacKenzie, please stay
And stain my dark grey colours with the pink of children!"

MacKenzie!
Will you stay?"

May

She was beautiful.
Her name was May.
So aptly chosen after a tropical summer's day-
With almond eyes that touched my infant heart.

She reached down to lift me from my infant cradle.
She smelled of cocoa beans; a scent of the earth.
Cocoa powder and my infant talcum mixed in sweet aroma.

My infant eyes observed her hands-
Fine and round; unlike a woman from the "squat-lands" bound.
They lifted me high into the air where I had never been before,
And on her bosom I gently lay
And there I nestled in and drowned in May.

She was ebony.
 I was ivory.
Talcum powder.
Cocoa butter.
Mixed with the island's sun together.
My black Madonna.
O how I loved her!

She left one day all dressed in white
An angelic sight-
In a dress my mother gave.
A young man took her away.
They looked similar
And smiled together.
He held her hand,
Her finger wore a golden band,

And they walked away.
And I never saw her to this day.

May!
My mother said I cried day after day.
I still remember May,
Beautiful May,
Who went away
As I in my cradle lay
On a summer's day
In May.

Memory

That dung-pile called *Memory*
Where like beetles we bury our dark brown lives;
Where we visit from time to time
To savour the odour of thoughts.

A moribund dwelling place-
An abandoned out-house
That *pit*
That *privy*
That *biffy*
Wherein we sneak in our *"nightsoil"*
Under the dark of night.
A *"thunderbox"*
A *"long-drop"*
To six feet
Where waste and worn out bodies meet.

That hut wherein we must enter
But to savour who we are,
Yet dread the dark, damp, awful smell of it all.

Memory-
Where we like dung- chafer- scarab
Roll our thoughts into neat tight balls,
And *tunnel* our deeds where only we can find
A dwelling place for our private lives of skulls and bones.

Memory.
Droppings beneath the *soul* of our shoe-
Remnants of remnants that remain
Cemented permanently.

A part of our *sole* being
Shaped into years and tears of travel along the refuse
We refuse to accept as our lives.

Here we wipe our *souls* at the edge of someone else's door,
And like the secret putrid sore
We visit in our mind,
We leave the smell of blame behind;
So that we in future time may find
Once more,
Waiting behind the Outhouse door-
-Memory;
Whore!

Morning Coffee

My first cup of coffee for this day in time.
How many more remains?
Are cups of coffee like grains of sand?
-Counting out our breaths in solemn sound.
A dark damp mound
Of spent grounds
Commended to the ever widening wound:
Dark
Dank
Damp
And dead
As lead.

My Brothers Young

My brothers young in the sap of their seed-
Sharp and stinging in the froth of youth,
No call nor need nor cause indeed
Could stay this running tribe of south.

My brothers strong in marrow and bone-
Tight and straight in the hip of life,
Their swagger and roll and their will of stone
Laid waste to all that dared make strife.

My brothers' hearts that's full of wonder-
And souls made mellow by the sweet law,
Whose fertile minds would wrestle and ponder
On life's mysterious folds would gnaw.

My brothers! Hearts tender to the feel-
Their laughter like cannons in the valley,
Slow to kneel and bold of zeal
My brothers' years in scores now tally.

"Where have all my brothers gone?
Now that all their deeds are done,
I miss their boyish ways and laughter
Alas! There is none to call my brother"

My Wish

May you ride
The tide
In bold blood,
And may your fortune flood
The full seas of your quest;
And then to rest
Having stood the test,
Blessed, Bless-ed, Blest.

Native Man

Native man
Native-man.
Tepee bedding in the city's roar,
Joseph's coloured coat coloured no more.

Native man.
Perched on his concrete throne,
No drum, no song, he sits alone.
Native-man
Native bone
Native stone.

Native man.
At the corner of the market place,
Crossed legged,
Hunched over,
An open palm his Princely mace.

Native man.
Native son.
Beneath the legs of passersby,
His world a quartered tent devoid of sky.

Native man
Native drum.
Native hum.

Native boy
Turned *"injun toy"*,
Warmed by the prison bars,
Smoked by the subway tunnel,

Nailed to the iron crate
Peace-pipe and funnel.

Native brother-
Flesh and iron fused together,
Ancient blood pouring down the sewer.

Now

There is no past!
-Just the present in reverse.
There is no future!
-Just an overly presumptuous now.
As for the now-
"What now?"

Old Age

We bow in reverence to the omniscience of old age;
Fierce and stern and unforgiving
He stands knee deep in our private memories
And bathes us in regrets.

He buries us in scabs and fallen hair
And brittle bones that grind to powdered blood.

Old age, cunning old age,
Drags us collared deep into a sea of tears
And drowns us in the rising tide,
Where Methuselah stands waiting-
Unimpressed.

Mockingly-
Old age hands us the sun which was our life's chase,
Which rays he knows we cannot feel.

Old age tempts us with tomorrow's dawn
Which he knows we cannot rise to meet.

Old age challenges us with sky and a thousand stars
Which he knows our remaining years cannot count.

Old age seduces us with young round hips
And laughs at our awkwardness.

Bored-
He hauls us away
Without a line to end the play;

Deep into the fog
Without an epilogue.

On Visiting an Old Relative

I laid my hands upon his head
  As we sat on his bed:

"All my friends are dead", He said,
"All my friends are dead!"
"John and Sue and Sidney too"
Mary, Bill and Lou".

"All the boys are gone", He said
He smiled and hung his head,
"So sad to hear, Ken, my friend so dear"
"Passed away last year".

"And Bill, to visit me one day
"Sometime in early May,"-
"At 92 he went away"
"He had a good long stay."

"Do you remember Raymond? Ray!"
"He lived at 20 Downing"
"-I saw him silently hauled away"
"One grey November morning"

"And Joe, Yes Joe! A joyful happy fellow-"
"Full of life and youthful callow-"
"Hit by a car at Cortege Lane-
"Some say he felt no pain."

"All my Pals have left,
Now I am all bereft"
 "All the gang is dead. "He said,

His words ran quick across the bed,
Grey and dank and dead as lead.

"Ah! Yes! My fragrant Heather
"Her smile I do remember"-
"We went to school together"-
"My pretty sweet and scented Heather"-
"With Heather-
"It was always kissing weather!"

"And Neville"
"Oh he was quite a devil!"
"Full of mischief"
"Full of life,"
"In the bottle he sure did revel."
"Even he!
-"The mighty Neville,"
"Who seemed invincible,"
"Lies upon the crosses knee"
"Amidst the graveyard's rubble."

Sad threnody! Too much to tell!
I rose with last farewell, I said-
"I'll be back to see you soon"
"We'll have lunch at noon"
-

"No! No! "He said,
"There's no more parting word to tell:
- "My final Angelus at noon!
"The sun now hides within the well"
"And night gives up the moon."

I heard him mumble deep and low
Laid back on his pillow-
-*"My friends drink deep amongst the Willow,*
"They call and I must follow"

I rose and kissed him on the brow,
He looked me in the eye,
I knew this was his final bow
Our last and fond goodbye.

I left him sitting on his bed,
All final words now said-
God gave to him one day to live-
My long last relative.

On Your Birthday

The years have flown my friend,
And you and I together face the stoop of age.
Whatever life hugs along its sightless bend,
This wish for you I do commend:
"Sweet contentment of well lived years,
The dimming of life's pain and cares,
The quiet wisdom of the sage
Then the graceful turning of a page."
Ah! Yes, the years have flown my friend,
But this simple pledge I do defend-
A faithful heart unto the end.

Owl

A wild wanton nest of feathers
Crouched at the north nib corner of my balcony-
Speckled brown and grey against the heavy stone.

Perched in prayer,
Poised in prescience,
Praised in princely presence to
Eyes of Wisdom; shutters closing in time,
Drawing the curtain on eons with a wink.

Restful in repose,
He chose my throne-
Dense and cold in humble stone,
Though barren and unforgiving
In its embrace of the North wind.

From night's dark world,
From forest to urban bower,
From bough and tree
To concrete tower,
He turned his head to gaze at me.

A feathered windmill
Cold and chill
In wisdom's spill.
Wise and wild
Moanful and moody,
This soldier of the night
With eyes of the moon
Sucked dry from me all vanity.

For I knew from this creature:
What he had seen,
Where he had been,
My human heart will fail to venture.

Prayer
While Crossing a Stream in Spring

"If this be earth!"
O what *Empyrean* bliss must then be held in store for man;
That in haste of life we have forgotten.

Here we wept as captives over *Edom*
And sang our song to *Zion*.

But when the cloud of misty closings guide us home
To David's throne,
We will remember who we are-
Children of the *Magen David* Star;
As we cross this earthly stream
In *Yohu'shuah* heart and blood redeem.

Promise of the Rainbow Through My Tears

"I did not steal your ten pence Madam"
"I did not break the Law,"
Nor violate the *eighth* command
It was not me you saw.
T'was someone else who stole your pence
Why must I bear the sentence?
Have I not suffered enough shame?
Why must I bear the blame?

I did not steal the ten pence Lady
I can plead no more,
Before you knot the noose make ready-
Please listen I implore:
"I was out amongst the woodlands"
"Frolicking in the trees"
"I was laughing with the blue birds,"
"Comforted by a breeze"

But who cares about my innocence,
Who ponders on my pain?
Who shares my burdened penance?
-Truth's defender slain!
Who walks with me towards the gallows?
Save the roll of salted sea-
That starts from deep within heart's hollows
And billows torrent free.

I rise to face the dawn's sunlight
That soothes my childhood sentence,
And feel the slip twist swift and tight
The knot that burns my innocence.

My eyes in flood Baptismal sight
Through tender childhood fears-
Cascades of multicoloured *light-*
"The promise of the rainbow through my tears"

She

She is head
   He is heart
Together in need
   Forever a part

Of the same that keeps them apart.

She is joint
   He is nerve
Away from the point
   Together they swerve

Losing their balance at the endless curve.

She is bow
   He is arrow
The joint that bends the bow
   The nerve that flings the arrow

Searching for the heart through bone and marrow.

She is thought
   He is feeling
Her reason caught
   By his ever seeking

Singing the same song without the rhyming.

She is sunlight
        He is moon-ray
She lights the day
        He kindles the night

When the moon appears the sun takes flight.

Her seasons changing
        His rain keeps falling
Northern winter snowing
        Summer roses dying

The sun condemning-
        Moon to the gallows hanging.

She Left but Her Space Remains
Hallucinating at coffee the day after

She left!
But her space remains-
A vagrant shadow in memory's bosom,
Greeting me in the kitchen the day after;
Moving near the coffee pot in the corner where we sat.
Then in a moment, gone.
Exorcised by the incense of sharp espresso.
Pouring into single Uno
No longer Duo.

It is back!
Her space.
Remembering the dark rhythm in the pour
In three quarter time
Not a single drop more.
One sugar for her two sugars for me,
I remember-Tuesday she had Green Tea?
Today? Coffee-
Even though her cup is empty.
Then the stir
And her purr
In quiet contentment-
Arabica Espresso our morning sacrament.
The chiming of spoon at the bell of her cup-
Stirring memories.
Digging out dark sugars.
That sharp ring of bells with rhythm all its own
Counting out memories that together we had sown.

Now it moves into the "dining" room ahead of me,

And crosses its leg in her favourite chair,
And we sip the dark sweet blood together
One quiet sip after another.

There it moves again!
With the fragrance of yesterday's perfume-
That deep stirring odour of desire
That a woman carries with her-
No scent can equal hair and flesh together.

It moves and sits beside me
And holds my hand upon her knee.

This wild wraith from my freshly dug past
Between my place and her space –
Corporeal! Incorporeal?

The dead lead thud of an overcooked soul
Laid in the trough the empty cup and bowl.

She left-
But her space remains.
Sweet absence stains.

Her coffee grounds.
Two freshly dug mounds.

Her moving space
Her sounds.

Simplicity

Laughter un-puckers the sphincter of life,
Tears grease the flow of feeling;
Love stems the tide of strife,
Smiles knead the balm of healing.

Smile

Lips:
A slit at dawn
A sear at morn
A slice at noon
A crescent moon
A silken seam
A rosy beam
A split at even
A glimpse at heaven
A slender tether
A shudder
A sip to savour
A spilling over
A quiver
A fissure
A tremor
A gentle scour
An open pore
A silent sear
A tender tear
A scented sever
A spill of laughter
A quiet thunder

"Her smile"!

So Much

We have so much that we are now in need,
And need so much that we fail in deed
To feed
And share
And pay out rightful fare.

Something Sweet and Charming

There is something sweet
Though sad and charming about good-byes.

They trap a moment's intense storm-
Severe and full of every taste of living
In a swift, quick thrust of a dagger:
A burn,
Clean
Crisp
And coring.

An ending
A surviving,
A coping
And telling
Of a new beginning-
Lurking somewhere
In that dizzying moment's imbalance,
Caught in the vise of starting over.

Stopping at the American Cemetery
Chaguaramas, Trinidad.

In the shade of the bamboo
    As the sun lit the west,
The boys from the Bayou
    Laid their heads to rest.

-In the land of the Chaguaramas.

Crying crosses
    Losing form forlorn,
Stooping crosses
    Of souls long gone.

-In the land of the Cumana.

Eyes of white
    Skin of Khaki,
Boots sewn tight
    By the hand of the Yankee.

-In the land of the Aracuas.

The arms are all gone
    Yet the arms remain,
Their deeds are all done
    And their crosses lain.

-Claimed by the Kingdom of Hyarima

Swimmer

The water nymph that in the virgin's evening hour-
When the sun retires and the moon stands guard in the tropic
bowl-
Slides silently on.

Slicing the water's face in even ripples;
Turning east then west,
A Half faced Cygnini,
She cavorts gracefully with the evening sky.

With a shoulder roll she sets up her gaze at the moon
And a shadow of a smile, red lipped and luscious
Catches a solitary intrusive beam of light,
As she glides seductively along.

From my balcony,
Stirred in wonder at her youth and form
I watch; as Acis dances gracefully:
Parsifal's lamentation,
Lohengrin's chariot,
Galatea-
She performs perhaps for me.

One curve of a hip,
One turn of an arm
Catching the moons gaze,
Causing a sigh and ripple to blush in the heavens.

Her perpetual circles and turns leave a scented scene behind to
savour.

Then gone as she came-
The dying swan leaving her watery wake to awaken my desire.

And I add my tear to the water's face
In tribute to her style and grace,
And mourn her swan's farewell.

The End of Things

The end of things ends with such an abrupt ending.
So much pain is endured to arrive at this spot,
But when the end comes it ends with a dot.
We dribble through living
Like the slow pus of a boil-
Oozing.
Bent by burden, torn by toil
And writhing in a tangled knot
In *coolie* Gavotte.
Then, the end comes as a royal Prince!
Taking all the glory that we have claimed since
We began this dance
-This *Totentanz*.
That impudent end,
Brazen and bold,
Cheats us of our prize
To savour the size
Of our own demise.

The Last Rose in Her Garden

The last Rose in her garden now pressed between the quires of a book,
Faded testimony of love now hushed.
Faded pink and gentle-
Petals dried as bones.
And through its faded veins of yesteryear I see our lives:
Viewed memories,
Sweet remembrances!
Tender embraces,
Tasted kisses.

An ocean of memories-
A mountain of hair.
A valley of desire.
A plain of hunger.
A river unquenched-
Meandering through my heart building up deep, sweet sediment.

The Rose was once bright pink like an unsolicited kiss-
The bright pink of promise.
The treasure unopened.
Now a letter sealed in fragrance-
So antiseptic in its greeting,
But guided by true sentiment so tender and tearful
It read:
"The last Rose in My Garden".
Now it lays dead and dry and without feeling.

Should it be moistened with a tear?
Or left to sear
The pages of the heart.

The stem through all this time stayed green-
Eternity's eager fuse always set to rekindle the scene.
A savoured smell,
An empty well
Where dry leaves fell;
To a sarcophagus-tiny and lonely
Climbing a wall on the garden fence.

I remember where it grew-
Upon the sheltered shelf near the red brick;
And how she cared for it.
She would rub its petals the way she rubbed my cheek.
She would tousle the leaves the way she tousled my hair
And stop to curl them around her fingers.
All that remains of that rose bush is -
"The last Rose in my garden"!

Caught like a vise between the pages of my book-
Tiny and lonely.
Squeezed into lifeless form-
All sap and substance
And Juices drained,
A scab remained
Where once an open wound ran rich and red and full of the pink
That lovers drink.

Now:
A sad flower,
For a sad time
In a sad rhyme.

Forever torn between time and circumstance-
Eternally trapped between leaf and flower,
A rose bush torn from a scented arbour.

I closed the book.

I buried it amongst the many library books-
A decaying memory too painful to remember

Perhaps one day
Before the petals decay,
I will try to find it once again-
"The Last Rose in My Garden".

The Month of May

"Welcome!"-spoke a stranger's hand
That early morn in May,
When he embraced his new found land
These forty years to stay.

It was the month of May some forty years today.

"I do!"He cried his sooth,"I do!"
To pledge his love in May,
And turned to meet the woman who
Some twenty years he lay.

It was the month of May some twenty years today.

He rose to meet the infant morn
Within the birth of May,
He held his cherub sweet fine born
These thirty years he lay.

It was the month of May some thirty years today.

He broke his oath and did depart
On one sad day in May,
And turned his eyes to new found heart
Another twenty years in May.

It was the month of May some two score years today.

But it was not to be this way,
She turned his love away.
He fled amongst sad tears of grey

And watched her love decay.

It was the month of May some twenty years today.

Now he lies amongst the tomb stones grey
In quiet restful play,
And watch another sun in May
Swing fast across the bay.

Now unremembered and forgotten since he passed this way in
May.

The Old Hindu Man

The Old Hindu Man lives one hundred miles away from me,
I am 1106,
He is 1103.
His walking time holds eons from his door to mine,
As I hear his shuffle past my door at nine.

A weather vane he is; I can tell from his vest,
As he dances his head from a sunken chest-
To attest-
"Perhaps you see, the wind is blowing"
"And a distinct possibility of much snowing"

He is a gentle man this Hindu soul,
The click of his door closes in his smell-
I can tell; he is a gentle mole
Never a sound from his prison cell.

Sometimes on a still grey morning,
His incense knocks at my door,
And with resonant moan in Sanskrit chanting,
Makes its way down the hallway along the floor.

"And a most joyful and splendiferous day to you young man!"
Says he; with the raise of his hand,
And with his cane as a wand,
He would bless me with a glance
In *Mahatma's* stance.

The old Hindu Man now lives in a different time from me,
Gone to join his aged ancestry,
But I still hear his shuffle past 1103
And his quiet blessings of," *Om Shanti Shanti!*"

The Quarrel

It began with a bicker-
I can hardly remember;
Perhaps a silly thoughtless comment
That fomented to ferment.

"I really don`t remember
What I said to offend her."

Yet it fell
        to a cavil,
                Then slid to a carp;

                              It rose to a quarrel,
        Sanguine and sharp.

"Still I don't remember
What I said to offend her."

Yet it sizzles in a squabble
                Now it boils in a fray-
And simmers

       in a wrangle,

           I`m- unsure —what- to —say!

*"I **t r u l y** don`t remember*
What led to her distemper."

If only I knew
How to sweeten this brew?

I would give her the spring
If only I could bring
Back, her sweet kisses
Instead of her hisses

*"I honestly **don`t** remember*
What I said to displease her,
Not even recall-
*What **led** to this brawl?"*

Then her sharp words cut through bone and gut
And I bled in her fading sight.

The Willow Under My
Window Bids Me Good Night

The Willow under my window bids me good night,
And we both wonder;
Will we see each other in the morning's light?
She looks up at me, high above her head,
And I look down at her settled quietly amongst the Maple and
Spruce;
Superior in my view but submissive to her splendour-
Brave and gallant in her embrace of winter's might.

She looks so mournful; folding in her arms.
Her Christed head hangs to one side against a fragile shoulder,
And I whisper:
"Good night dear friend, do not weep for me."

Hold tight your sap for the winter's rage,
Look to the Maple that wise old sage
Who sleeps between the winds and sleet,
Anchored sure and deep upon his feet.

Rest your gentle leaves upon night's windy pillow
And sleep for soon the spring will follow;
And you and I will meet once more,
Under my window in the winter's thaw.
Here we will laugh and sing
And tell of dreams that the spring will bring.

Until then my Woeful Weeping Willow,
We sleep until the spring's tomorrow.

There is an Unsettling in the Heavens

There is an unsettling in the Heavens.

Uranus scowls!

The *Horai* in disagreement
Have left Olympus Gates unguarded.

And the Seasons slink away without goodbye.
One season gone in a day.
In a moment's leaving
Surrendering night to tomorrow's dawn.

The Autumn,
Unprepared for the rage of Winter-
Implores the sleeping *Polyphemus:*
His eye now closed-
Vanquished by *Pomona's* dance.

Seduced by the soft white curves of winter's snow-
Chilled and huddled without a shawl,
Looking for the puzzled moon to intervene-
Spring and summer banished from the garden green,
Naked and unseen.

Scattered stars in disarray
Hurry away.

The North wind jostles the South
For its place between the seasons.

The dawn rises questioningly,

"When did the Summer leave"? She moans.
So soon?
The moon

Challenging the night sky-
Astronomy where and why.

The almanac,
Carried away by the man
In the moon
With the sack
On his back.

Array in disarray:
September's Summer,
October's Winter,
Pandora's innocence
Now mankind's penance.

Horai stands defeated at the Garden tomb,
While *Vertimnus* lays within *Pomona's* barren womb.

Summer calls from Winter's Hall,
The Spring falls in ruptured *caul*
From Autumn's Wall.

There is an unsettling in Heaven-
The Blood all riven.

Neither God nor men
     Can ever mend it again.

There is still so much to see

"Go away!
"Let me *be.*"
"There is still so much to see"
"Much thought and will that's left in me"

A single star that lights the sky,
A gentle creek that babbles by.
A fresh and new born infant's smile,
A bushel of apples in a red pile.
"Go away!
"Just let me be,"
"There is still much love that's left in me"
"Will you go away Mefistofele"?

I glimpse the Red Tide across the Cay.

But there is still in me much of the sea
That sprightly innocence of childhood glee,
To watch the birth of wave upon the sand,
Testing the shore with an orphan's hand.

Now, unsure of strange embrace to welcome or repel,
My once mighty wave now modest in its swell.

"Please go away!
"-Too soon! Too soon!"
Sea lice nests under the waxing Gibbous Moon.
I know there's still much left in me,
A Viking Langskip worthy of the warring sea.

"Will you go away?"
-"At least for a small bouquet of seasons."
-"Perhaps a *ha'penney* of years"
"Can we bargain in reasons?"
"Can we barter in tears?

I promise to measure and treasure
Simple pleasure:
The sound of the brook
Through inlet and nook,
Its bicker and babble
With the rock as its saddle.
-The infant's gurgle
A saintly chuckle-
An unwritten symphony
Void of brass and timpani.

"Will you *then* go away?"
"For just the longest day?"
"-Give me time to kneel and pray!"

"What do you say?"
"Is it yea or nay?

"I see! I see!"
You answer me;

It comes! This wraith-
This rolling lathe,
The ebbing sea."

You then decline
This plea this pine,
You toast my tongue with bitter brine-
No Sacramental drop of rich red wine!

Then grant me this last simple line.
"To hug once more this boy of mine."

Time to Go

Time to go!
Another beckons-
A passing on to new trails.

I have dwelt long and deep in the place of green winds
And full tides;
Bounding to the roll of harmony's ring-
To the edge of sweetness full and round
And dripping with the sap of song.

I have savoured:
The roar of rhythm,
Tear of tune,
Volley of voice,
Soaring to the summit of suns
And the root of notes.

Deep and wide I have tended tears
And lived fears
With the text of giants and the sigh of Gods.

Now! It is time to go.
Another beckons-
A passing on to new hearts on the winds of curve
And on melody's lips; kissed forever by my sighs
And buried deep down in harmony's hearth.

I turn the corner:
Embrace the curve,
Round the bend,
Skip the wave,
Stand up from the heart to gaze on all I feel,
Leaving behind my song on memory's heel.

To John

Another leaf has fallen from your tree,
But in its place a sweeter richer fruit is born to be.
You no longer count your years in numbered tally,
But in its stead a rolling sea of memory.

Be brave in the hours of silver thought,
For in your hands did many a kindness wrought.
We do remember all that in your tender years did sow,
But we in younger sibling ways could not find ways to show.

It was upon your young shoulders
Where many a task and weighty burden laid-
Still merely a man but much a father then,
You carried the yoke of all and ten.

Be brave in the hour of aging deeds,
Because of your gifts we crept onward as young steeds.
And now old salts, we sailed way round the world,
Sailing home to port our sails unfurled.

Together a crew, united we sail once more
My friend, my brother, to greener shore;
Where we can watch the sunsets turn
And view the skies a golden urn.

And when the mist of God descends,
Together, our father's seeds ascend.
Be brave in the hour of shortened breath and final gong,
We are one blood, one heart, one soul, one song.

Tomorrow

Tomorrow
Will I rise to meet another dawn?
-The dark night's curtain having now been drawn.
As I slumber in a web of dreams-
Is it my choice?
Do I possess the means
To light another candle,
To birth another ray?
Can it be my doing as I lay-
Having slain another day,
To rise and face the hunter's horn
And chase the shadowy night into a fresh new morn?
Or will tomorrow's sun bier another soulful mourn.
Is it my choice to greet another dawn?
If then this voice be mine
To score this final line,
Then I think I'll keep the curtains drawn.

Truant Boy

Down at the slipway on a summer's day
Where the boats gave way to the murky bay,
He would spend all day in play
And watch the boats across the way.

This truant boy would sit and play
And sail play boats across the bay,
And at noon when the sun moved high-
Would watch the corbeaux in the sky.

Then crabs would venture out to feed
From slime and mud and rotted seed-
Eyes first then heads then edged claw
Would drag what's dead upon the shore.

Then he would pile the shells and stones
In rows upon the dead fish bones,
And count the tiny fish that swim
And learn the many colours limn.

This boy dreamt dreams of time unseen
To places he had never been,
And wait under the cherry tree
For the horn to set the shore-men free.

A signal time for him so soon
To follow them to lunch at noon.
Then books so carefully to stack,
For after lunch he would be back.

The truant boy saw things serene,

Grown men had never ever seen:
The gull that dove deep in the bay
To hold its breath and savour prey.

The pelican on half a leg
Would beg its food from turtle egg,
The oyster scarce that moved a breath
But siphoned life from waters depth.

This truant boy learnt lessons well
More than any school could tell:
From simple act as why leaves fell
To what gave rise to the sea swell.

School laid no rule to what was best
Nor made a claim to formal test-
No pen to scribe an elegy
Of sky or wave nor silent sea.

He watched the sea give way to shore,
The shore give way to sea.
The wind that whip and wail and roar
Then sleep upon the island's knee.

When in the west the sun had hailed
And all his childhood boats had sailed,
He gathered up his books and stool
And headed homeward bound from school.

"What did you learn today at school"?
His father questioned as a rule;
He thought of stones and bones and shell
And answered, "I learnt my sums so well"

"What more was taught at school today?"
His father then would say:
The boy replied," Much Geography
About the Island's fish and sea"

"And ships of different nationality-
"Taught me much of history"
"And yes, the leaf from off a tree"
"Taught me much biology"

"What lessons did you like the least?"
His father smiled to give a test,
Well, he thought of Geography
But shouted out," Astronomy!"

 "Why so my tired little rover?"
His father waited for the answer-
"Why, when the moon begins to hover"
"The sun says that my school is over".

Watching a Woman Walk By

Mysteriously,
She sails by, bone slack,
Hips pitching in a rolling wave.

Then, with a shiver, she stops-
Caught in a tide of thought.
She trims her sails with a tight tug at her canvas;
Jibing her fore-and-aft for eyes to feast-
Yet her cargo of desire rolls on,
Destined to somewhere we'll never know.

Then she turns about-
A starboard tack,
A stack
Of hips,
That breathless hum of a woman in full sail;
Beckoning, but unreachable as the rolling reeds in an inviting
lake,
Leaving in her wake
Untold desires.
A folded thigh laid out for all to see,
The white flash of a turning knee,
At her cheek, the tear of a teasing smile-
Her hair a flare
In quick affair at our stare,
Knowing what we feel.

Then dissolved,
Eclipsed,
Gone!
Sinking over the horizon;
Leaving all bereft save the sight of her keel
And the rosy glimpse of a parting heel.

When Darkness Falls!

When does darkness fall
Can you recall
The very second when things cease to be visible?
Are they visible in one blink
And invisible the next?
Or, do they just fade gradually-
From sunlight's blaze
To a gloomy haze?

The darkness must be there; all wrapped in a shell
Waiting for the tide to begin its swell.
Does it move in an invisible dance?
Covering our eyes in a webbed trance.

Can you see the deceitful darkness
 Before it wraps its arms around a sunny day?
Can you taste the old wine when the cask is still young?
-The old must be there with its taste on the tongue.
If lips became false when kisses are true
Can you savour the flavour before the brew?

As darkness snuffed the candle's glow
It bled in waxen tears of sorrow.
"Yes, I failed to see the sunlight fade,
Nor did I feel the creeping shade.
I died within her parting shadow,
She left no trace for me to follow

Now, ask me, "Do you remember when darkness fell?"
"O Yes I do; and I can tell"
"For now I know it well!"

When It Is Time to Leave

When it is time to leave behind
    The love that I once knew,
And summon up the sweet courage
    To bade a sad Adieu.

To face the death of faithful friend
    And sing a fond farewell,
Then bow in sweet contented praise-
    Last music sounds now swell.

This faithful friend who walked with me
    Through storm and lilting day,
Must now be placed as relic old,
    In vault of dust and clay.

Both faithful friend and kindly foe-
    A duo on the stage,
Now stands between the curtain wings
    And see me turn the page.

So long dear friend, my gentle foe,
    Together we have fought-
Together we have loved and laughed-
    The strains of music sought.

Each note each rest each waiting breath,
    A strict and comrade bold,
Now it is time to cut the chord
    And let the banner fold.

Let us leave our notes to echo
  And leave our voice to cheer,
Let us hug the dark blue curtain
  And turn without a tear.

I will remember you dear friend
  In turn remember me.
Our hearts as rich as meadows gold
  And drunk with memory.

Now grasp my final outstretched hand
  Our final note intones,
Then lay be down in Muse's gown
  Between the tear stained stones.

Come! Lend me Hermes Sacred Lyre
  And Apollo's fluted tones,
Clothe me in the robes of Sparta
  Now! Light the Pyre o'er my bones.

Alphabetical List Of First Lines

AUTHOR BIOGRAPHY

Richard Claude Valdez was born in Port-of-Spain, Trinidad, the third of nine children born to Imogene(Jean) Atkinson and Francisco(Frank) Vicente Valdez. Early in his childhood, the family Valdez moved to the northern hills of suburban Cascade, where he lived until he immigrated to Toronto, Canada in 1970. In Trinidad, Richard grew up amongst nature. His landscape and playmates were the trees, birds, tropic rains, blue skies, starry nights and long stretching sea shores, washed by the waters of the Caribbean Sea and the Atlantic Ocean. Many of these images are reflected in his poems. His first volume of poetry entitled, Aperture, was published in 2009.

He resides in Toronto, Canada and in Florida, with frequent visits to his island home of Trinidad.